Panini, bruschetta & crostini

Panini, bruschetta & crostini

Simply delicious recipes for classic Italian toasted and open sandwiches

RYLAND PETERS & SMALL

LONDON • NEW YORK

Designer Emily Breen
Production Mai-Ling Collyer
Art Director Leslie Harrington
Editorial Director Julia Charles
Publisher Cindy Richards

Published in 2017 by Ryland Peters & Small
20-21 Jockey's Fields
London WC1R 4BW
and
341 E 116th St
New York NY 10029
www.rylandpeters.com

Text © Maxine Clark, Jennifer Joyce, Laura
Washburn and Ryland Peters & Small 2017
Design and photographs © Ryland Peters
& Small 2017

ISBN 978-1-84975-817-8

A catalogue record for this book is available from
the British Library. US Library of Congress CIP
data has been applied for.

Printed in China

Notes

- Both British (metric) and American (imperial plus US cup) measurements are included in these recipes for your convenience, however it is important to work with one set of measurements only and not alternate between the two within a recipe.
- All spoon measurements are level unless otherwise indicated.
- All eggs are medium (UK) or large (US), unless otherwise specified. Uncooked or partly cooked eggs should not be served to the very young, the very old, the frail, pregnant women or those with compromised immune systems.
- When a recipe calls for the grated zest of citrus fruit, buy unwaxed fruit and wash well before using.
- Ovens should be preheated to the specified temperatures. We recommend using an oven thermometer. If using a fan-assisted oven, adjust temperatures according to the manufacturer's instructions.

contents

toast with taste ...

There is something quintessentially Italian about toasted and open sandwiches. The word panini translates as 'little breads' but it encapsulates a whole variety of tasty sandwiches with melting cheese, traditional hams, spicy salami, grilled chicken, delicious fish and all manner of vegetables appearing as mouthwatering fillings.

The cooking method for panini is simplicity itself. Most of the recipes take just 3 minutes in a panini press, or you can use a stovetop ridged grill pan instead and cook the sandwiches for a couple of minutes on each side.

Bruschetta and crostini have become firm favourites in our modern lifestyles, appearing at smart dinner parties as appetizers and at cocktail parties as pre-dinner nibbles – far removed from their humble peasant origins, but none the worse for that.

Bruschetta is good crusty Italian bread, toasted over a wood fire or cooked on an iron stovetop grill pan, then rubbed with garlic and anointed with olive oil. Bruschetta can be finished with the simplest tomato topping or crowned with luxuries such as shrimps, chicken, mushrooms or perfectly grilled vegetables.

Crostini, on the other hand, are smaller, more refined snacks, usually baked in the oven or fried until crisp. These are elegantly served with pre-dinner drinks and are frequently offered as a matter of course in Italian bars. Crostoni, just larger crostini, are nice and crunchy, and vehicles for any combination of ingredients. In the northern regions of Italy, particularly the Veneto, crostini are made using fried or grilled/broiled polenta as the base.

Whether its a simple lunch, a casual supper, part of an antipasti selection or an appetizer for an Italian meal, there is nothing more Italian than the simplicity of panini, bruschetta and crostini.

the basics

True bruschetta (and it is pronounced 'brooskayta' not 'brooshetta') is a large slice of country bread toasted on the barbecue or over a wood fire and then rubbed with garlic, sometimes topped with a crushed tomato and anointed with olive oil. It is a popular snack found all over Italy, served in bars and at home. A true crostoni (large) or crostini (small) is brushed with olive oil and cooked in the oven or under the grill/broiler, or fried in olive oil or butter.

bruschetta

4 thick slices country bread, preferably
  sourdough
2 garlic cloves, halved
extra virgin olive oil, for drizzling

SERVES 4

Grill/broil, toast or pan-grill the bread on both sides until lightly charred or toasted. Rub the top side of each slice with the cut garlic and drizzle with olive oil. Keep warm in a low oven before adding your chosen topping.

crostini

1 Italian sfilatino* or thin French baguette
extra virgin olive oil, for brushing

SERVES 6

* A sfilatino is a long, thin loaf available from Italian delicatessens and larger supermarkets.

Preheat the oven to 190°C (375°F) Gas 5. Slice the bread into thin rounds, brush both sides of each slice with olive oil and spread out on a baking sheet. Bake for about 10 minutes until crisp and golden. Let cool, then keep in an airtight container until ready to use. It is best to reheat them in the oven before adding the topping. Crostoni are simply cut from a larger loaf and prepared in the same way as crostini.

polenta crostini

300 g/2 cups polenta flour
extra virgin olive oil, for brushing, or butter, for frying

SERVES 6–8

Make the polenta by slowly sprinkling the flour into 1 litre/quart of salted, boiling water. Cook over a low heat for 45 minutes, stirring occasionally. Turn out into a mound onto a wooden board. Let cool and set. Alternatively, use the quick-cook version (cook according to the manufacturer's instructions), or even the ready-made kind sold in a block. Slice the cooled and set polenta into the thickness you want, and cut or stamp out the required shape and size. Melt a little butter in a hot, non-stick frying pan/skillet and cook until crisp, turning once. Alternatively, brush both sides with olive oil or melted butter and cook on a stove-top grill pan, turning once, if you prefer a char-grilled taste.

Vegetali Vegetables

egg, mushroom, havarti and dill panini

asparagus, fontina and sun-blush tomato panini

garlic greens and provolone panini

gruyère, cheddar and spring onion/scallion panini

courgette/zucchini, red onion and goat's cheese panini

roasted fennel, tomato, fontina and pesto panini

portobello mushroom, taleggio and pesto panini

char-grilled aubergine/eggplant, ricotta and sun-blush tomato pesto panini

caramelized onion, gorgonzola, rosemary and watercress panini

marinated artichoke, olive and provolone panini

pear, pecorino and pea crostini

slow-roasted tomatoes on bruschetta with salted ricotta or feta

egg, mascarpone and asparagus crostini

cherry tomato, bocconcini and basil bruschetta

white bean and black olive crostini

traditional peasant tomato and garlic bruschetta (fettunta)

olive oil and garlic bruschetta

artichoke, pesto and pine nut bruschetta

goat's cheese and sweet red peppers on bruschetta

garlic mushrooms with gremolata on bruschetta

baba ganoush crostini topped with crispy aubergines/eggplants

cherry tomato bruschetta

Danish Havarti is a mild yet tangy cheese that works particularly well with mushrooms. Sliced Emmental or Gouda would also be tasty in this panino.

egg, mushroom, havarti and dill panini

1 ciabatta loaf
180 g/1½ cups white button
   mushrooms, wiped and
   sliced
2 eggs, beaten
80 g /3 oz. Havarti cheese,
   thinly sliced
2 teaspoons chopped dill
sea salt and freshly ground
   black pepper
vegetable oil, for frying
   and brushing

MAKES 2 PANINI

Preheat a panini press. Cut the top and bottom off the ciabatta so that it is about 3 cm/1 inch thick. Save the crusts for another use. Slice open lengthways and then cut in half.

Heat 1 tablespoon of oil in a frying pan/skillet. Season the mushrooms with salt and pepper and gently fry for 4 minutes. Remove the mushrooms from the pan and set aside. Add another teaspoon of oil to the pan, pour in the eggs and scramble them over low heat. Evenly distribute the cheese between the two sandwiches. Spoon on the scrambled egg, top with the mushrooms and sprinkle with dill. Brush both sides of the panini with a little oil and toast in the preheated panini press for 2–3 minutes, or according to the manufacturer's instructions. The bread should be golden brown and the filling warmed through.

Serving suggestion: Serve this satisfying panino with a generous dollop of gourmet tomato or mushroom ketchup.

Fontina is a creamy, nutty cheese from the mountains of Italy that melts like a dream.

asparagus, fontina and sun-blush tomato panini

1 ciabatta loaf
10 asparagus spears
100 g/3½ oz. Fontina
cheese, grated
10 sun-blush tomatoes
or Roasted Tomatoes
(see page 138)
sea salt and freshly ground
black pepper
olive oil, for frying and
brushing

MAKES 2 PANINI

Preheat a panini press. Cut the top and bottom off the ciabatta loaf so that it is about 3 cm/1 inch thick. Save the crusts for another use. Slice open lengthways and then cut in half.

Heat a little oil in a frying pan/skillet. Add the asparagus, season with salt and pepper and fry for about 3 minutes. Divide the asparagus, cheese and tomatoes between the two sandwiches. Brush both sides of the panini with a little oil and toast in the preheated panini press for 2–3 minutes, or according to the manufacturer's instructions. The bread should be golden brown and the filling warmed through.

Serving suggestion: This is delicious drizzled with a little good-quality balsamic vinegar.

Any type of green, including kale or Swiss chard, can be used in this recipe. It's important to blanch even tender greens before searing in garlic, as this removes any bitterness. Ricotta or Gorgonzola would work nicely in place of the Provolone.

garlic greens and provolone panini

1 ciabatta loaf
100 g/2 cups spring greens, roughly chopped
2 tablespoons olive oil
1 garlic clove
a pinch of dried chilli flakes/hot pepper flakes
60 g/2½ oz. Provolone cheese, sliced
sea salt and freshly ground black pepper
vegetable oil, for brushing

MAKES 2 PANINI

Preheat a panini press. Cut the top and bottom off the ciabatta so that it is about 3 cm/1 inch thick. Save the crusts for another use. Slice open lengthways and then cut in half.

Blanch the greens in salted water for 2 minutes and then drain. In a frying pan/skillet, heat the olive oil. Add the garlic and chillies. Drop the greens in and season with salt and pepper. Toss for a minute and remove from the heat. Divide the greens between the two sandwiches and top with the cheese. Brush both sides of the panini with a little oil and toast in the preheated panini press for 2–3 minutes, or according to the manufacturer's instructions. The bread should be golden brown and the filling warmed through.

Serving suggestion: Serve this panini with a red and yellow tomato salad with sliced spring onions/scallions.

This is no ordinary toasted cheese sandwich. The mixture of Swiss Gruyère and mature Cheddar with spring onions/scallions is pure heaven.

gruyère, cheddar and spring onion/scallion panini

4 slices sourdough bread
50 g/2 oz. Gruyère cheese, grated
50 g/2 oz. mature/sharp Cheddar cheese, grated
2 spring onions/scallions, thinly sliced
sea salt and freshly ground black pepper
vegetable oil, for brushing

MAKES 2 PANINI

Preheat a panini press. Lay the slices of bread out. Divide the cheeses between the two sandwiches, add the spring onions/scallions, and season with salt and pepper. Put the tops on. Brush both sides of the panini with a little oil and toast in the preheated panini press for 2–3 minutes, or according to the manufacturer's instructions. The bread should be golden brown and the filling warmed through.

Serving suggestion: Try this panino with a dollop of grainy mustard on the side for dipping and a baby spinach salad.

Courgettes/zucchini are transformed by char-grilling as their flavour intensifies and becomes sweeter.

courgette/zucchini, red onion and goat's cheese panini

1 ciabatta loaf
2 small courgettes/zucchini, cut lengthways into slices ½ cm/¼ inch thick
8 thinly sliced rings of red onion
1 tablespoon freshly chopped mint
2 handfuls of rocket/arugula
100 g/3½ oz. firm goat's cheese, crumbled
sea salt and freshly ground black pepper
olive oil, for brushing

MAKES 2 PANINI

Preheat a panini press. Cut the top and bottom off the ciabatta so that it is about 3 cm/1 inch thick. Save the crusts for another use. Slice open lengthways and then cut in half.

Brush the courgettes/zucchini with a little oil and season with salt and pepper. Grill them for 1–2 minutes in the preheated panini press or a ridged stovetop grill pan. Divide the courgettes/zucchini between the two sandwiches. Top with the onions, mint and rocket/arugula, finishing with the cheese. Brush both sides of the panini with a little oil and toast in the preheated panini press for 2–3 minutes, or according to the manufacturer's instructions. The bread should be golden brown and the filling warmed through.

Serving suggestion: Try this panino with some slices of fresh radish on the side and a drizzle of balsamic vinegar.

If you don't have time to make roasted fennel and tomatoes, try an Italian deli for substitutes such as char-grilled courgettes/zucchini or aubergines/eggplants, or marinated 'antipasti-style' mushrooms.

roasted fennel, tomato, fontina and pesto panini

1 ciabatta loaf
2 tablespoons Basil Pesto
  (see page 139)
6 Roasted Tomatoes
  (see page 138)
4 slices Roasted Fennel,
  roughly chopped
  (see page 138)
80 g/3 oz. Fontina or
  mozzarella cheese, sliced
vegetable oil, for brushing

MAKES 2 PANINI

Preheat a panini press. Cut the top and bottom off the ciabatta so that it is about 3 cm/1 inch thick. Save the crusts for another use. Slice open lengthways and then cut in half.

Spread the pesto on the inside of both sandwiches. Place 3 tomatoes and 2 slices of fennel on each. Top with equal amounts of cheese. Brush both sides of the panini with a little oil and toast in the preheated panini press for 2–3 minutes, or according to the manufacturer's instructions. The bread should be golden brown and the filling warmed through.

Serving suggestion: Try this panino with a small bowl of peperoncini (pickled hot peppers), the Giardiniera (pickled vegetables) on page 140 or a simple cherry tomato and fresh basil salad.

Who needs meat when you have Portobello mushrooms? The texture of these large mushrooms is chewy, and they're surprisingly filling, particularly when smothered with tangy Taleggio cheese.

portobello mushroom, taleggio and pesto panini

1 ciabatta loaf
2 tablespoons Basil Pesto (see page 139)
4 large Portobello mushrooms, stems removed
2 tablespoons balsamic vinegar
100 g/3½ oz. Taleggio cheese, sliced
sea salt and freshly ground black pepper
olive oil, for brushing

MAKES 2 PANINI

Preheat a panini press. Cut the top and bottom off the ciabatta so that it is about 3 cm/1 inch thick. Save the crusts for another use. Slice open lengthways and then cut in half.

Spread the pesto on the inside of each. Brush the mushrooms with oil and drizzle with balsamic vinegar. Season with salt and pepper and grill for 1–2 minutes in the preheated panini press or a ridged stovetop grill pan. Place a mushroom in each sandwich and top with the cheese. Brush both sides of the panini with a little oil and toast in the preheated panini press for 2–3 minutes, or according to the manufacturer's instructions. The bread should be golden brown and the filling warmed through.

Serving suggestion: Try this panino with the Saffron Garlic Mayonnaise on page 141.

There is a big difference between supermarket ricotta and what you will find in an Italian deli. The latter is fresh, creamy and glorious with char-grilled aubergine/eggplant.

char-grilled aubergine/ eggplant, ricotta and sun-blush tomato pesto panini

1 ciabatta loaf
2 tablespoons Sun-blush Tomato Pesto (see page 139)
1 medium aubergine/ eggplant, cut into slices ½ cm/¼ inch thick
2 tablespoons balsamic vinegar
2 tablespoons freshly chopped basil
8 thinly sliced rings of red onion
60 g/2½ oz. ricotta cheese
sea salt and freshly ground black pepper
olive oil, for brushing

MAKES 2 PANINI

Preheat a panini press. Cut the top and bottom off the ciabatta so that it is about 3 cm/1 inch thick. Save the crusts for another use. Slice open lengthways and then cut in half.

Spread the pesto on the inside of both the sandwiches. Brush the aubergine/eggplant slices with some olive oil and balsamic vinegar and season with salt and pepper. Grill the slices for 1–2 minutes in the preheated panini press or a ridged stovetop grill pan. Roughly chop them and divide between the sandwiches. Top with the basil and onion slices and finish with the ricotta. Brush both sides of the panini with a little oil and toast in the preheated panini press for 2 minutes, or according to the manufacturer's instructions. The bread should be golden brown and the filling warmed through.

Serving suggestion: Try this panini with a leafy green salad.

Spicy watercress is ideal for panini. Like rocket/ arugula, and unlike most other salad leaves, it isn't too too watery and provides the perfect peppery punch.

caramelized onion, gorgonzola, rosemary and watercress panini

1 ciabatta loaf
4 tablespoons Caramelized
   Onions (see page 140)
1 teaspoon freshly chopped
   rosemary
2 handfuls of watercress
40 g/1½ oz. Gorgonzola
   cheese, sliced
40 g/1½ oz. Fontina or
   mozzarella cheese, sliced
vegetable oil, for brushing

MAKES 2 PANINI

Preheat a panini press. Cut the top and bottom off the ciabatta so that it is about 3 cm/1 inch thick. Save the crusts for another use. Slice open lengthways and then cut in half.

Place the onions in both the sandwiches and sprinkle with rosemary. Top with watercress and then finish with the cheeses. Brush both sides of the panini with a little oil and toast in the preheated panini press for 2–3 minutes, or according to the manufacturer's instructions.

The bread should be golden brown and the filling warmed through.

Next time you feel the need for pizza, try this instead.
Most of the ingredients are pantry staples, so leaving
the house to make it may not even be necessary. This
is perfect when you need something tasty in a hurry.

marinated artichoke, olive and provolone panini

4 slices panini bread
1–2 tablespoons sun-dried
   tomato paste
180 g/6 oz Provolone, grated
   or thinly sliced
6–8 marinated artichokes,
   drained and sliced
65 g/½ cup pitted/stoned
   green olives, coarsely
   chopped
½ teaspoon dried oregano
unsalted butter, melted,
   for brushing

SERVES 2

Preheat a panini press. Brush butter on the bread slices on one side. Spread two of the slices with sun-dried tomato paste on the non-buttered side and set aside.

Top the other two slices of bread with half of the cheese. Arrange the artichokes on top and sprinkle with the olives and oregano. Sprinkle over the remaining cheese and cover with the other bread slices, tomato side down.

Toast in the preheated panini press for 2–3 minutes, or according to the manufacturer's instructions. The bread should be golden brown and the filling warmed through.

Cut each panino into quarters before serving.

A wonderful combination of fresh spring flavours and colours. Puréeing the peas gives a sweet, earthy base on which to sprinkle the combination of salty, nutty Pecorino (Parmesan would work very well here, too) and fruity pears tossed in a few drops of balsamic vinegar for sharpness. A delicious start to a light dinner party.

pear, pecorino and pea crostini

1 Italian sfilatino or thin French baguette, sliced into thin rounds

250 g/2 cups shelled fresh or frozen peas

freshly grated nutmeg

1 small ripe pear

a drop of balsamic or sherry vinegar

125 g/4 oz. fresh young Pecorino or Parmesan cheese, diced

sea salt and freshly ground black pepper

extra virgin olive oil, for brushing and moistening

SERVES 6

Preheat the oven to 190°C (375°F) Gas 5. To make the crostini, brush both sides of each slice of bread with olive oil and spread out on a baking sheet. Bake for about 10 minutes until crisp and golden.

Meanwhile, blanch the peas in boiling water for 3 minutes if they are fresh or 2 minutes if they are frozen. Drain them, refresh in cold water and drain again. Purée the peas in a food processor or blender, moistening with a little olive oil. Season with salt, pepper and freshly grated nutmeg.

Core and finely chop the pear. Mix with a drop of balsamic or sherry vinegar, then add the cheese and mix well.

Spread the crostini with a mound of pea purée and top with a spoonful of the pear and cheese mixture. Serve immediately.

These firm but juicy roasted tomatoes burst with the flavour of the sun. They take no time to prepare but a long time concentrating their flavours in the oven – they smell fantastic while cooking! Plum tomatoes have less moisture in them and work well. You can use other vine-ripened varieties – just make sure they have some taste!

slow-roasted tomatoes on bruschetta with salted ricotta or feta

8 large ripe plum tomatoes
2 garlic cloves, finely
 chopped
1 tablespoon dried oregano
4 tablespoons extra virgin
 olive oil
50 g/2 oz. salted ricotta or
 feta cheese, thinly sliced
sea salt and freshly ground
 black pepper
basil leaves, to serve
 (optional)

FOR THE BRUSCHETTA:
4 thick slices country bread,
 preferably sourdough
2 garlic cloves, halved
extra virgin olive oil, for
 drizzling

SERVES 4

Preheat the oven to 170°C (325°F) Gas 3. If using plum tomatoes cut them in half lengthways, if using round ones cut them in half crossways. Put them cut-side up on a baking sheet. Mix the garlic and oregano with the olive oil, salt and pepper. Spoon or brush this mixture over the cut tomatoes. Bake for about 2 hours, checking them occasionally. They should be slightly shrunk and still a brilliant red colour. If they are too dark they will be bitter. Let cool.

To make the bruschetta, grill, toast or pan-grill the bread on both sides until lightly charred or toasted. Cut the bruschetta slices to size so that 2 tomato halves will sit on top of each one. Rub the top side of each slice with the cut garlic, then drizzle with olive oil.

Put 2 tomato halves on each bruschetta, sprinkle with the thinly sliced cheese and top with a basil leaf, if you like. Serve the bruschetta at room temperature.

This is a creamy light topping, packed with the flavour of asparagus. For the best results, don't be tempted to make this with anything other than fresh asparagus. If you have some, you can drizzle a little truffle oil over for a special occasion, as the flavours of eggs and truffle go very well together.

egg, mascarpone and asparagus crostini

1 Italian sfilatino or thin French baguette, sliced into thin rounds

125 g/4 oz. unsalted butter, softened

4 tablespoons freshly chopped parsley

4 spring onions/scallions, finely chopped

12 spears fresh green asparagus, stems trimmed

6 large/US extra-large eggs

4–6 tablespoons mascarpone cheese, softened

sea salt and freshly ground black pepper

extra virgin olive oil, for brushing

truffle oil, for drizzling (optional)

SERVES 6

Preheat the oven to 190°C (375°F) Gas 5. To make the crostini, brush both sides of each slice of bread with olive oil and spread out on a baking sheet. Bake for about 10 minutes until crisp and golden.

Meanwhile, beat the butter with the parsley and spring onions/scallions, and season with salt and pepper.

Cook the asparagus in boiling salted water for about 6 minutes until tender. Cut off and reserve the tips and slice the stems.

Boil the eggs for 6–8 minutes. Plunge into cold water for a couple of minutes, then shell and roughly mash with a fork. Add the spring onion/scallion mixture and mascarpone and stir until creamy. Fold in the sliced asparagus stems, then season with salt and pepper.

Spread the egg mixture thickly onto the crostini, top with the asparagus tips and drizzle with a couple of drops of truffle oil, if using, or some extra virgin olive oil. Serve immediately.

All the colours of the Italian flag are here – red, white and green. This makes a great start to a rustic summer meal. Bocconcini (meaning 'little bites') are tiny balls of mozzarella. They are the perfect size for bruschetta but, if you can't find them, use regular mozzarella instead and cut it into cubes.

cherry tomato, bocconcini and basil bruschetta

4 tablespoons extra
  virgin olive oil
1 teaspoon balsamic
  vinegar
12 bocconcini, halved,
  or 375 g/13 oz.
  mozzarella, cubed
20 ripe cherry
  tomatoes or
  pomodorini (baby
  plum tomatoes),
  halved
a handful of basil
  leaves, torn, plus
  extra to serve
125 g/1 cup rocket/
  arugula
sea salt and freshly
  ground black pepper

FOR THE BRUSCHETTA:
4 thick slices country
  bread, preferably
  sourdough
2 garlic cloves, halved
extra virgin olive oil,
  for drizzling

SERVES 4

Whisk 3 tablespoons of the olive oil with the balsamic vinegar. Season to taste with salt and pepper. Stir in the halved bocconcini or mozzarella cubes, tomatoes and torn basil.

To make the bruschetta, grill, toast or pan-grill the bread on both sides until lightly charred or toasted. Rub the top side of each slice with the cut garlic, then drizzle with olive oil.

Cover each slice of bruschetta with rocket/ arugula and spoon over the tomatoes and mozzarella. Drizzle with the remaining olive oil and top with fresh basil leaves.

The combination of bland creamy beans and sharp, rich, salty tapenade makes a sublime mouthful, especially on crisp crostini.

white bean and black olive crostini

FOR THE TAPENADE:
175 g/6 oz. Greek-style black olives, such as Kalamata, pitted
2 garlic cloves
3 canned anchovies, drained
2 teaspoons capers, drained
1 tablespoon olive oil

FOR THE CROSTINI:
1 Italian sfilatino or thin French baguette, sliced into thin rounds
extra virgin olive oil, for brushing

FOR THE WHITE BEAN PURÉE:
2 tablespoons olive oil
2 garlic cloves, finely chopped
1 teaspoon very finely chopped fresh rosemary

1 small red chilli/chile, deseeded and finely chopped
400 g/14 oz. canned cannellini beans, rinsed and drained
sea salt and freshly ground black pepper

TO SERVE:
freshly chopped parsley

SERVES 6–8

To make the tapenade, put the olives, garlic, anchovies, capers and olive oil into a blender or food processor and blend until smooth. Scrape out into a jar, cover with a layer of olive oil and set aside.

Preheat the oven to 190°C (375°F) Gas 5. To make the crostini, brush both sides of each slice of bread with olive oil and spread out on a baking sheet. Bake for about 10 minutes until crisp and golden.

Meanwhile, make the bean purée. Heat the oil in a small frying pan/skillet and add the garlic. Cook gently for 2 minutes until golden but don't let it turn brown. Stir in the rosemary and chilli/chile. Remove from the heat, add the beans and 3 tablespoons of water. Mash the beans roughly with a fork and return to the heat until warmed through. Taste and season with salt and pepper.

Spread a layer of tapenade on the crostini followed by a spoonful of bean purée. Sprinkle with chopped parsley and serve immediately.

The word fettunta comes from the Tuscan dialect and derives from latin, meaning 'anointed slice'. It is a slice of bread grilled over hot coals, rubbed with garlic and drizzled with olive oil. To be authentic you should use only the finest Tuscan extra virgin olive oil. The ripe tomato is traditionally crushed in your hand and smashed onto the bread, then eaten immediately, but this is a more civilized version.

traditional peasant tomato and garlic bruschetta (fettunta)

4 large very ripe tomatoes
4 thick slices country bread, preferably sourdough
2 garlic cloves, halved
sea salt and freshly ground black pepper
extra virgin olive oil, for drizzling

SERVES 4

Roughly chop the tomatoes and season with salt and pepper. To make the bruschetta, grill, toast or pan-grill the bread on both sides until lightly charred or toasted. Rub the top side of each slice with the cut garlic, then drizzle with olive oil.

Spoon the tomatoes over the bruschetta and drizzle with more olive oil. Eat immediately with your fingers!

This is pared-down simplicity and so easy to make. It beats the likes of doughballs and garlic bread hands down. The most important thing is not to overcook the garlic – it must on no account turn brown. This is great served instead of garlic bread with a selection of salads.

olive oil and garlic bruschetta

4 large garlic cloves
6 tablespoons extra virgin olive oil
a good pinch of dried chilli flakes/hot pepper flakes
4 tablespoons freshly chopped parsley (optional)

FOR THE BRUSCHETTA:
4 thick slices country bread, preferably sourdough
extra virgin olive oil, for drizzling

SERVES 4

Slice the garlic lengthways into paper-thin slices. Heat a small pan, pour in the olive oil and stir in the garlic. Cook until the garlic starts to give off its aroma and is golden but not brown (or it will taste bitter). Remove from the heat, then mix in the dried chilli flakes/hot pepper flakes and parsley, if using. Cover to keep warm.

To make the bruschetta, grill, toast or pan-grill the bread on both sides until lightly charred or toasted, then drizzle with olive oil. Spoon or brush over the garlicky spicy oil. Eat immediately with your fingers!

This is a joy to make when fresh artichokes are in season. If fresh ones are not available, you can use frozen, canned or those preserved in oil.

artichoke, pesto and pine nut bruschetta

6 small, fresh artichokes, each about 8 cm/3 inches long
2 tablespoons olive oil
25 g/2 tablespoons butter
1 tablespoon balsamic vinegar
4 tablespoons Basil Pesto (see page 139)
2 tablespoons pine nuts, toasted
shavings of Parmesan cheese

FOR THE BRUSCHETTA:
4 thick slices country bread, preferably sourdough
2 garlic cloves, halved
extra virgin olive oil, for brushing

SERVES 4

To make the bruschetta, grill, toast or pan-grill the bread on both sides until lightly charred or toasted. Rub the top side of each slice with the cut garlic, then drizzle with olive oil. Keep them warm in a low oven.

Prepare the artichokes (see note below) and cut them in half. Heat the oil and butter in a frying pan/skillet, add the artichokes and fry gently until they are completely tender and beginning to brown. Splash in the balsamic vinegar, turn up the heat and toss the artichokes until the vinegar evaporates.

Spread the bruschetta with the pesto and divide the artichokes between the slices. Sprinkle with the pine nuts and Parmesan shavings. Serve immediately.

Note: To prepare fresh artichokes, first fill a bowl with water and squeeze in the juice of half a lemon. Use the other lemon half to rub the cut portions of the artichokes as you work. Trim the artichokes by snapping off the dark green outer leaves, starting at the base. Trim the stalk to about 5 cm/2 inches and peel it. Cut about 1 cm/1/2 inch off the tip of the artichoke, then place them in the lemony water until required.

Cooked goat's cheese is a relative newcomer to Italian cuisine. When grilled/broiled, its sharp, creamy texture perfectly partners the smoky sweetness of roasted red peppers, especially when topped with salty, pungent capers and a little dressing.

goat's cheese and sweet red peppers on bruschetta

2 sweet red peppers
4 tablespoons Basil Pesto
  (see page 139)
8 thick slices goat's cheese
  with rind

FOR THE BRUSCHETTA:
4 thick slices country bread,
  preferably sourdough
2 garlic cloves, halved
extra virgin olive oil, for
  drizzling

FOR THE CAPER DRESSING:
2 tablespoons salted capers,
  soaked in water
for 10 minutes, then rinsed
  and chopped
3 tablespoons extra virgin
  olive oil
1 teaspoon balsamic vinegar
sea salt and freshly ground
  black pepper

SERVES 4

Preheat the oven to 240°C (475°F) Gas 9. Put the peppers into a large roasting pan and roast for 20–30 minutes, turning once, until they begin to char. Remove from the oven and put into a plastic bag, seal tightly and set aside for 10 minutes to steam off the skins. Meanwhile, to make the bruschetta, grill or pan-grill the slices of bread on one side only until lightly charred or toasted. Rub the grilled sides with the cut garlic, then drizzle with olive oil. Keep them warm in a low oven.

Remove the peppers from the bag and peel off the skins, then pull out the stalks – the seeds should come with them. Cut the peppers in half, scrape out any remaining seeds and slice the flesh thickly.

To make the caper dressing, put the chopped capers into a bowl, then stir in the olive oil, vinegar, salt and pepper.

Spread the pesto over the ungrilled side of the bruschetta and put 2 slices of cheese on each one. Cook under a preheated grill/broiler for 1–2 minutes or until the cheese is beginning to melt and turn golden (watch that the bread doesn't catch and burn).

Remove from the heat and put a tangle of roasted peppers on top and drizzle with the caper dressing. Serve immediately.

A grown-up version of mushrooms on toast. Don't be tempted to use button or shiitake mushrooms: the first are too bland, the second too strong. Try a combination of porcini and girolles or chanterelles.

4 thick slices country bread, preferably sourdough
melted butter, for brushing

FOR THE BLACK OLIVE GREMOLATA (OPTIONAL):
1 small garlic clove, finely chopped
finely grated zest of 1 lemon
4 tablespoons freshly chopped flat leaf parsley
16 Greek-style black olives, such as Kalamata, pitted and chopped

FOR THE GARLIC MUSHROOMS:
75 g/3 oz. butter or olive oil
3 shallots, finely chopped
2 garlic cloves, finely chopped
500 g/1¼ lb. large mushrooms, thickly sliced
5 tablespoons dry white wine
3 tablespoons freshly chopped flat leaf parsley
sea salt and freshly ground black pepper

SERVES 4

garlic mushrooms with gremolata on bruschetta

To make the bruschetta, preheat a stove-top grill pan, add the slices of bread and cook on both sides until barred with brown. Brush with melted butter and keep them warm in a low oven.

To make the gremolata, put the garlic, lemon zest, parsley and olives into a bowl, stir well, cover and chill.

Then, prepare the garlic mushrooms. Melt the butter or heat the olive oil in a frying pan/skillet, add the shallots and garlic and fry for 5 minutes until soft and golden. Add the mushrooms and toss well. Fry over high heat for 1 minute.

Add the wine and season with salt and pepper. Cook over high heat again until the wine evaporates. Stir in the parsley. Pile the mushrooms on the bruschetta and serve immediately, topped with a sprinkling of gremolata, if using.

Baba Ganoush is a Middle Eastern dip, usually served with a flatbread. It works well on crostini and could almost be Sicilian with its mixture of aubergine/eggplant and sesame seed flavours.

1 aubergine/eggplant, about 450 g/1 lb.

3 tablespoons tahini

1 garlic clove, crushed

a pinch of hot paprika, plus extra for serving

2 tablespoons freshly chopped parsley or coriander/cilantro

freshly squeezed juice of 1 lemon

3 large ripe tomatoes, very thinly sliced

sea salt and freshly ground black pepper

extra virgin olive oil, for drizzling

FOR THE CRISPY AUBERGINES/EGGPLANTS:

vegetable oil, for shallow frying

1 small aubergine/eggplant, very thinly sliced

FOR THE CROSTINI:

1 Italian sfilatino or thin French baguette, sliced into thin rounds

extra virgin olive oil, for brushing

SERVES 6

baba ganoush crostini topped with crispy aubergines/eggplants

Preheat a stovetop grill pan until very hot. Prick the aubergine/eggplant all over with a sharp knife, then pan-grill, turning regularly, until blackened and completely soft. This will take about 20 minutes. Let cool slightly, then remove the charred skin. Roughly chop the flesh, put it in a sieve/strainer and let drain. Press to remove the bitter juices.

Blend the aubergine/eggplant flesh in a blender or food processor with the tahini, garlic and hot paprika, then stir in the parsley or coriander/cilantro. Add lemon juice, salt and pepper to taste.

For the crispy aubergines/eggplants, heat the oil in a frying pan/skillet and add the sliced aubergine/eggplant. Cook until brown and crisp. Remove with a slotted spoon and drain on paper towels.

Preheat the oven to 190°C (375°F) Gas 5. To make the crostini, brush both sides of each slice of bread with olive oil and spread out on a baking sheet. Bake for about 10 minutes until crisp and golden.

Put a slice of tomato on each crostini, season with salt, then spoon on a mound of baba ganoush and top with a slice of crispy aubergine/eggplant. Drizzle with olive oil and sprinkle with hot paprika. Serve immediately.

Juicy tomatoes contrast nicely with the crunchiness of the baked bread in this vibrant, classic Italian snack. Serve as a rustic start to a meal, a midday snack or a lunchtime treat.

cherry tomato bruschetta

12 red and yellow cherry
   tomatoes, quartered
1 teaspoon olive oil
1 teaspoon balsamic vinegar
1 garlic clove, peeled
4–6 fresh basil leaves, plus
   extra to garnish
sea salt and freshly ground
   black pepper

FOR THE CROSTINI:
1 Italian sfilatino or thin
   French baguette, sliced
   into thin rounds
extra virgin olive oil, for
   brushing

MAKES ABOUT 12

Preheat the oven to 190°C (375°F) Gas 5. To make the crostini, brush both sides of each slice of bread with olive oil and spread out on a baking sheet. Bake for about 10 minutes until crisp and golden.

Meanwhile, mix together the cherry tomato quarters with the olive oil, balsamic vinegar, a pinch of salt and whole garlic clove in a large bowl. Shred the basil leaves and mix in. Set aside to allow the flavours to infuse while the baguette slices bake and cool.

Discard the garlic clove from the tomato mixture, then spoon onto each slice of bread. Garnish with basil leaves and sprinkle with pepper. Serve at once.

2

Pesce Fish

smoked salmon, cream cheese, tomato, onion and caper panini

•

tuna, celery, cheddar and sun-blush tomato on sourdough bread

•

mozzarella, anchovy, lemon and red onion panini

•

tuna, black olive, pine nut and caper crostini

•

spicy squid and aubergine/eggplant on bruschetta

•

spicy garlic shrimp with tomatoes and chickpeas on bruschetta

•

goujons of sole with watercress tartare crostini

•

smoked salmon and lemon pepper cream crostini

This classic combination of fillings, usually served in a bagel, becomes even more delicious when reinvented as a panino. A little peppery watercress or rocket/arugula makes a nice addition.

smoked salmon, cream cheese, tomato, onion and caper panini

1 ciabatta loaf
4 tablespoons cream cheese
4 slices of smoked salmon
1 teaspoon small capers
2 teaspoons finely diced
   red onion
1 plum tomato, deseeded
   and chopped
a small handful of
   watercress or rocket/
   arugula (optional)
sea salt and freshly ground
   black pepper
vegetable oil, for brushing

MAKES 2 PANINI

Preheat a panini press. Cut the top and bottom off the ciabatta so that it is about 3 cm/1 inch thick. Save the crusts for another use. Slice open lengthways and then cut in half.

Layer the fillings on the two sandwiches starting with the cream cheese, followed by the salmon, capers, red onion, tomato and watercress, if using. Season well with salt and pepper.

Brush both sides of the panini with a little oil and toast in the preheated panini press for 2–3 minutes, or according to the manufacturer's instructions. The bread should be golden brown and the filling warmed through.

Serving suggestion: Sprinkle with some freshly chopped dill.

Although you can of course use ciabatta, sourdough bread is a particularly good choice for this crunchy, easy-to-make sandwich.

tuna, celery, cheddar and sun-blush tomato panini on sourdough bread

4 slices sourdough bread
100 g/3½ oz. (drained
   weight) canned tuna
1 tablespoon diced celery
1 tablespoon finely diced
   red onion
4 tablespoons Homemade
   Mayonnaise (see page 141)
6 sun-blush tomatoes,
   drained
50 g/2 oz. mature/sharp
   Cheddar cheese, grated
sea salt and freshly ground
   black pepper
vegetable oil, for brushing

MAKES 2 PANINI

Preheat a panini press. Mix the tuna with the celery, onion and mayonnaise and season with salt and pepper. Divide the tuna mixture between the two sandwiches, top with tomatoes and add the cheese.

Brush both sides of the panini with oil and toast in the preheated panini press for 3 minutes, or according to the manufacturer's instructions. The bread should be golden brown and the filling warmed through.

This bold Sicilian trio of anchovy, garlic and lemon is just the right accent for creamy mozzarella.

mozzarella, anchovy, lemon and red onion panini

1 ciabatta loaf
2 tablespoons olive oil
2 garlic cloves, sliced
1 anchovy fillet, rinsed of oil
4 tablespoons freshly chopped parsley
grated zest of 1 unwaxed lemon
130 g/5 oz. (2 large balls) fresh buffalo mozzarella, sliced
4 tablespoons Caramelized Onions (see page 140)
vegetable oil, for brushing

MAKES 2 PANINI

Preheat a panini press. Cut the top and bottom off the ciabatta so that it is about 3 cm/1 inch thick. Save the crusts for another use. Slice open lengthways and then cut in half.

Heat the olive oil in a small frying pan/skillet. Add the garlic and anchovy. Cook until the garlic is golden and the anchovy starts to break up. Remove from the heat and add the parsley and lemon zest. Spread this mixture over the inside of both the sandwiches. Top with the cheese and caramelized onions.

Brush both sides of the panini with a little oil and toast in the preheated panini press for 2–3 minutes, or according to the manufacturer's instructions. The bread should be golden brown and the filling warmed through.

Serving suggestion: Serve this panino with a crisp raddichio salad.

The contrast of strong flavours and interesting textures in this recipe transports you instantly to the shores of the Mediterranean. Use a mixture of green and black olives if you prefer a sharper flavour. This mixture can be used as a stuffing for tomatoes, too.

tuna, black olive, pine nut and caper crostini

175 g/1½ cups oven-baked or Greek-style black olives, pitted and chopped

2 tablespoons pine nuts, chopped

1 tablespoon capers, rinsed and chopped

1 small garlic clove, finely chopped

1 tablespoon freshly chopped parsley

6 sun-dried tomatoes, soaked and chopped

1 tablespoon finely grated lemon rind

100 g/3½ oz. (drained weight) canned tuna in oil, drained

sea salt and freshly ground black pepper

extra virgin olive oil, for moistening

FOR THE CROSTINI:

1 Italian sfilatino or thin French baguette, thinly sliced diagonally

extra virgin olive oil, for brushing

SERVES 6

Preheat the oven to 190°C (375°F) Gas 5. To make the crostini, brush both sides of each slice of bread with olive oil and spread out on a baking sheet. Bake for about 10 minutes until crisp and golden.

Put the olives, pine nuts, capers, garlic, parsley, tomatoes and lemon rind in a bowl and mix well. Add the tuna, break it up with a fork and mix it thoroughly with the other ingredients. Moisten with a little olive oil, taste and season with salt and pepper. Pile the mixture on top of the crostini. Serve immediately.

spicy squid and aubergine/eggplant on bruschetta

450 g/1 lb. baby squid, cleaned and sliced (see note below)
1 small aubergine/eggplant, very thinly sliced
115 g/1 cup rocket/arugula
sea salt and freshly ground black pepper
vegetable oil, for deep-frying
lemon wedges, to serve (optional)

FOR THE MARINADE:
2 small red chillies/chiles, deseeded and chopped
2 garlic cloves
finely grated rind and juice of 1 lemon
1 tablespoon sugar
4 tablespoons olive oil

FOR THE BRUSCHETTA:
4 thick slices country bread, preferably sourdough
2 garlic cloves, halved
extra virgin olive oil, for drizzling

SERVES 4

To make the marinade, put all the ingredients into a blender or food processor and blend until smooth. Stir the squid into the marinade, cover and leave for 2 hours.

For the bruschetta, grill, toast or pan-grill the bread on both sides until lightly charred or toasted. Rub the top side of each slice with the cut garlic, then drizzle with olive oil. Keep warm in a low oven.

Preheat the vegetable oil for deep-frying in a wok or deep-fryer to 190°C (375°C) or until a piece of stale bread turns golden in a few seconds when dropped in. Deep-fry the aubergine/eggplant slices in batches until brown and crisp. Remove with a slotted spoon and drain on paper towels, then arrange in an even layer over the bruschetta. Keep warm in a low oven.

Heat a heavy frying pan/skillet until it is very hot and brush with oil. Remove the squid from the marinade and drain well, reserving the marinade. Sauté the squid for about 1 minute, tossing all the time until just caramelizing. Pour the marinade into the pan and boil rapidly for 30 seconds to reduce. Spoon the squid over the aubergine/eggplant slices. Serve immediately with some rocket/arugula piled on top and lemon wedges, if using.

Note: To clean fresh squid, pull the head from the body. Remove the plastic quill from the inside of the squid tube, then rinse the tubes. Trim the tentacles from the head. Pop out the beak from the centre of the tentacles. Rinse, discarding the head and entrails.

This is a very popular combination of ingredients in southern Italy. Sweet prawns and tomatoes contrast with earthy chickpeas, pungent garlic and a hint of fiery chilli. Great food for warm summer evenings in the garden.

spicy garlic shrimp with tomatoes and chickpeas on bruschetta

2 tablespoons extra virgin olive oil
2 garlic cloves, finely chopped
½ teaspoon dried chilli flakes/hot pepper flakes
100 ml/⅓ cup dry white wine
225 g/½ lb. ripe tomatoes, peeled and chopped, or canned tomatoes, chopped
½ teaspoon sugar (optional)
200 g/7 oz. raw, shelled prawns/shrimp

4 tablespoons canned chickpeas, rinsed and drained
2 tablespoons freshly chopped flat leaf parsley
sea salt and freshly ground black pepper

FOR THE BRUSCHETTA:
4 thick slices country bread, preferably sourdough
2 garlic cloves, halved
extra virgin olive oil, for drizzling

SERVES 4

Heat the oil in a large frying pan/skillet and add the garlic. Fry until just turning golden then add the chilli flakes/hot pepper flakes and wine. Turn up the heat and boil fast to reduce the wine to almost nothing. Add the tomatoes (if you are using canned tomatoes add some sugar to bring out their flavour) and cook for 1–2 minutes until they start to soften. Stir in the prawns/shrimp and chickpeas and bring to the boil. Simmer for 2–3 minutes. Stir in the parsley, taste and season with salt and pepper. Set aside.

To make the bruschetta, grill, toast or pan-grill the bread on both sides until lightly charred or toasted. Rub the top side of each slice with the cut garlic, then drizzle with olive oil. Spoon over the spicy garlic prawn/shrimp mixture and serve immediately.

225 g/½ lb. thick sole fillets, skinned
2 tablespoons seasoned flour
1 egg, beaten
50–100 g/½-1 cup breadcrumbs, toasted
sea salt and freshly ground black pepper
vegetable oil, for deep-frying
watercress sprigs and lemon wedges, to serve

FOR THE CROSTINI:
1 Italian sfilatino or thin French baguette, sliced into thin rounds
extra virgin olive oil, for brushing

FOR THE WATERCRESS TARTARE SAUCE:
50 g/½ cup watercress leaves, blanched, squeezed dry and very finely chopped
300 ml/1¼ cups mayonnaise
1 teaspoon freshly chopped tarragon
2 tablespoons freshly chopped parsley
1 tablespoon capers, rinsed and chopped
2 tablespoons chopped gherkins

SERVES 6

Crunchy sole and homemade tartare sauce.

goujons of sole with watercress tartare crostini

Preheat the oven to 190°C (375°F) Gas 5. To make the crostini, brush both sides of each slice of bread with olive oil and spread out on a baking sheet. Bake for about 10 minutes until crisp and golden. Let cool, then keep in an airtight container until ready to use. It is best to reheat them in the oven before adding the topping.

Cut the sole fillets diagonally across the grain into thin strips. Toss the fingers in the seasoned flour and shake off the excess. Dip the sole fingers into the beaten egg in batches, turning them until well coated. Give them a bit of a shake, then toss in the breadcrumbs until evenly coated. Put them on a tray, making sure they don't touch, cover them with clingfilm/plastic wrap and refrigerate.

To make the tartare sauce, beat the watercress into the mayonnaise then fold in the tarragon, parsley, capers and gherkins. Taste and season well with salt and pepper.

Preheat the vegetable oil in a wok or deep-fat fryer to 190°C (375°C) or until a piece of stale bread turns golden in a few seconds when dropped in. Fry the sole sticks in batches until crisp and golden. Drain on paper towels, then sprinkle with salt.

Spread the crostini with a good dollop of tartare sauce, then top each one with 2 or 3 sole sticks. Serve with a few sprigs of watercress and some lemon wedges.

This makes an elegant alternative to the usual smoked salmon canapés. The cream has a punchy pepper kick to it with cool lemon undertones. Tossing the salmon in the dill gives it a lovely fresh appearance.

smoked salmon and lemon pepper cream crostini

225 g/½ lb. thinly sliced
   smoked salmon
2 tablespoons freshly
   chopped dill
sea salt

FOR THE CROSTINI:
1 Italian sfilatino or thin
   French baguette, thinly
   sliced diagonally
extra virgin olive oil, for
   brushing

**FOR THE LEMON PEPPER
   CREAM:**
2 teaspoons black
   peppercorns
75 ml/⅓ cup mascarpone
   cheese
75 ml/⅓ cup milk
finely grated zest and
   freshly squeezed juice
   of 1 lemon

SERVES 6

Preheat the oven to 190°C (375°F) Gas 5. To make the crostini, brush both sides of each slice of bread with olive oil and spread out on a baking sheet. Bake for about 10 minutes until crisp and golden. Let cool, then keep in an airtight container until ready to use. It is best to reheat them in the oven before adding the topping.

To make the lemon pepper cream, pound or grind the peppercorns as finely as possible. Beat the mascarpone with the ground pepper, add the milk and lemon zest and beat again. Season with salt and lemon juice to taste. Chill until needed.

Toss the smoked salmon with the chopped dill. Spread the crostini with the lemon pepper cream and place a mound of smoked salmon on top. Squeeze over a little more lemon juice and serve immediately.

3

Carne e pollame Meat & Poultry

egg, bacon, spinach and cheddar panini

bacon, potato and red leicester panini with tabasco sauce

serrano, goat's cheese, fig jam and rocket/arugula panini

salami, provolone, artichoke and peperoncini panini

chorizo, mozzarella, piquillo pepper and rocket/arugula panini

bresaola, artichoke, parmesan and rocket/arugula panini

sausage, mozzarella, roasted (bell) peppers and caramelized onion panini

pancetta, goat's cheese and sun-blush tomato panini

mortadella, provolone and giardiniera panini

pepperoni, mozzarella, black olive and pesto panini

pancetta, gorgonzola and apple panini

roast beef, caramelized onion, watercress and horseradish panini

prosciutto, balsamic fig and fontina panini

salami, roasted fennel, fontina and caper panini

turkey, gruyère, jalapeño and mustard panini

chicken, gouda and red onion panini with honey-mustard dressing

chicken, scamorza, roasted tomato and watercress panini

pan-grilled chicken and guacamole on crisp polenta crostini

grilled fig and prosciutto bruschetta with rocket/arugula

chorizo with crunchy saffron potatoes on bruschetta

prosciutto-wrapped bocconcini crostini

carpaccio of beef with salsa verde on bruschetta

italian sausage with radicchio and taleggio on crisp polenta crostoni

mozzarella in carozza

meatball panini with tomato sauce and fontina

philly cheese steak panini

This is a grown-up and far more sophisticated version of a bacon-and-egg sandwich. A handful of fresh spinach cuts through the richness of the bacon and cheese, adding a healthy touch.

egg, bacon, spinach and cheddar panini

1 ciabatta loaf
6 rashers/slices bacon
2 eggs, beaten
1 large handful of baby spinach leaves
80 g/3 oz. mature/sharp Cheddar cheese, thinly sliced
sea salt and freshly ground black pepper
vegetable oil, for brushing

MAKES 2 PANINI

Preheat a panini press. Cut the top and bottom off the ciabatta so that it is about 3 cm/1 inch thick. Save the crusts for another use. Slice open lengthways and then cut in half.

In a frying pan/skillet, fry the bacon until crisp. Remove the bacon from the pan and discard most of the oil. Pour in the beaten egg, season well with salt and pepper and let the eggs set like an omelette/omelet.

Divide the spinach between the two sandwiches. Top with the crispy bacon, then half of the omelette/omelet and finish with the cheese. Brush both sides of the panini with a little oil and toast in the preheated panini press for 2–3 minutes, or according to the manufacturer's instructions. The bread should be golden brown and the filling warmed through.

Serving suggestion: If you like a hot chilli/chili sauce, such as Tabasco, try sprinkling some over this panino to give it an extra flavour kick.

Save your leftover baked or roasted potatoes to create this satisfying breakfast panino.

bacon, potato and red leicester panini with tabasco sauce

1 ciabatta loaf
6 rashers/slices smoked bacon
1 large cooked potato, sliced
50 g/2 oz. Red Leicester or Monterey Jack cheese, thinly sliced
2 teaspoons Tabasco sauce
sea salt and freshly ground black pepper
vegetable oil, for frying and brushing

MAKES 2 PANINI

Preheat a panini press. Cut the top and bottom off the ciabatta so that it is about 3 cm/1 inch thick. Save the crusts for another use. Slice open lengthways and then cut in half.

Add a little oil to a frying pan/skillet and fry the bacon until crisp. Remove from the pan and drain on paper towels. Keep the pan hot, add the potato slices and season with salt and pepper. Fry on both sides until crisp around the edges. Divide the bacon and potatoes between the two sandwiches. Add a dash of Tabasco sauce and top with cheese.

Brush both sides of the panini with a little oil and toast in the preheated panini press for 3 minutes, or according to the manufacturer's instructions. The bread should be golden brown and the filling warmed through.

The sweet-and-sour fig jam suits the salty air-dried ham and creamy goat's cheese perfectly. You could try other fruit jams such as quince or even a tomato chutney.

serrano, goat's cheese, fig jam and rocket/arugula panini

1 ciabatta loaf
4 tablespoon good-quality fig jam
4 thin slices Serrano ham or prosciutto
100 g/3½ oz. firm goat's cheese, crumbled
2 small handfuls of rocket/arugula
vegetable oil, for brushing

MAKES 2 PANINI

Preheat a panini press. Cut the top and bottom off the ciabatta so that it is about 3 cm/1 inch thick. Save the crusts for another use. Slice open lengthways and then cut in half.

Spread the fig jam on both sandwiches and top with the ham, goat's cheese and rocket/arugula. Brush both sides of the panini with a little oil and toast in the preheated panini press for 2–3 minutes, or according to the manufacturer's instructions. The bread should be golden brown and the filling warmed through.

Serving suggestion: Try this panino with the Smoky Paprika Mayonnaise on page 141 for dipping or, to make a more substantial meal, serve it with a chicory and walnut salad simply drizzled with vinaigrette dressing.

Provolone is the golden yellow, often pear-shaped, cheese seen hanging from a waxed string in Italian delis. It has a sharp, smoky taste and melts beautifully.

salami, provolone, artichoke and peperoncini panini

1 ciabatta loaf
6 pieces of marinated
  artichoke
8 slices Napoli Piccante or
  other Italian salami
10 peperoncini (pickled hot
  peppers) or pickled
  peppadews, drained
2 tablespoons Basil Pesto
  (see page 139)
80 g/3 oz. Provolone cheese
vegetable oil, for brushing

MAKES 2 PANINI

Preheat a panini press. Cut the top and bottom off of the ciabatta so that it is about 3 cm/1 inch thick. Save the crusts for another use. Slice open lengthways and then cut in half.

Layer the fillings in the two sandwiches, starting with the artichoke, followed by the salami, peppers, pesto and finishing with the cheese. Brush both sides of the panini with a little oil and toast in the preheated panini press for 2–3 minutes, or according to the manufacturer's instructions. The bread should be golden brown and the filling warmed through.

Serving suggestion: Try the Lemon and Fennel Seed Mayonnaise on page 141 for dipping. Serve with a simple green side salad, dressed with balsamic vinegar.

Spanish smoked paprika (pimentón) gives chorizo its characteristically rich, deep taste. Although you could use ordinary roasted peppers, do try to locate authentic piquillos as they are smoked in wood-burning ovens which gives them a flavour that is truly delectable.

chorizo, mozzarella, piquillo pepper and rocket/arugula panini

1 ciabatta loaf
4 whole piquillo peppers
(or other small roasted
red peppers), drained
12 slices chorizo sausage
2 handfuls of rocket/arugula
130 g/5 oz. (2 large balls)
fresh buffalo mozzarella,
drained and sliced
vegetable oil, for brushing

MAKES 2 PANINI

Preheat a panini press. Cut the top and bottom off the ciabatta so that it is about 3 cm/1 inch high. Save the crusts for another use. Slice open lengthways and then cut in half.

Layer the fillings in the two sandwiches, starting with the peppers, followed by the chorizo and rocket/arugula, finishing with the cheese. Brush both sides of the panini with oil and toast in the preheated panini press for 3 minutes, or according to the manufacturer's instructions. The bread should be golden brown and the filling warmed through.

Serving suggestion: Try making the Saffron Garlic Mayonnaise on page 141 and serve it on the side for dipping.

Bresaola is a salt-cured, air-dried beef fillet from Lombardy in the north of Italy. It is sold in most supermarkets these days but if you can't find it, thin slices of roast beef would work here, too.

bresaola, artichoke, parmesan and rocket/arugula panini

1 ciabatta loaf
8 slices bresaola
6 pieces marinated artichoke
4 tablespoons grated Parmesan cheese
8 thinly sliced rings of red onion
2 handfuls of rocket/arugula
70 g/2½ oz. (1 ball) fresh buffalo mozzarella, drained and sliced
vegetable oil, for brushing

MAKES 2 PANINI

Preheat a panini press. Cut the top and bottom off the ciabatta so that it is about 3 cm/1 inch high. Save the crusts for another use. Slice open lengthways and then cut in half.

Layer the fillings on the two sandwiches starting with the bresaola, then the artichokes, Parmesan, onion and rocket/arugula, finishing with the cheese. Brush both sides of the panini with oil and toast in the preheated panini press for 3 minutes, or according to the manufacturer's instructions. The bread should be golden brown and the filling warmed through.

Serving suggestion: For extra flavour, drizzle this panino with a little good-quality balsamic vinegar.

Chunks of pepper and deliciously spicy Italian sausage are married with oozing mozzarella in this unforgettable panino.

sausage, mozzarella, roasted (bell) pepper and caramelized onion panini

1 ciabatta loaf
3 Italian sausages, casings removed
4 tablespoons Caramelized Onions (see page 140)
4 tablespoons chopped roasted or char-grilled red (bell) peppers
130 g/5 oz. (2 balls) fresh buffalo mozzarella, drained and sliced
vegetable oil, for frying and brushing

MAKES 2 PANINI

Preheat a panini press. Cut the top and bottom off the ciabatta so that it is about 3 cm/1 inch high. Save the crusts for another use. Slice open lengthways and cut in half.

Heat a little oil in a frying pan/skillet and fry the sausage meat until crispy. Drain on paper towels and divide between the sandwiches. Top with onions, peppers and then the cheese.

Brush both sides of the panini with oil and toast in the preheated panini press for 3 minutes, or according to the manufacturer's instructions. The bread should be golden brown and the filling warmed through.

Use the firm-rinded goat's cheese here as it melts more slowly than the soft variety.

pancetta, goat's cheese and sun-blush tomato panini

1 ciabatta loaf
6 slices of pancetta or other unsmoked bacon
100 g/3½ oz. firm goat's cheese, crumbled or sliced
2 tablespoons chopped peperoncini (pickled hot peppers) or peppadews
2 handfuls of rocket/arugula
8 sun-blush tomatoes, drained of oil
vegetable oil, for frying and brushing

MAKES 2 PANINI

Preheat a panini press. Cut the top and bottom off the ciabatta so that it is about 3 cm/1 inch high. Save the crusts for another use. Slice open lengthways and then cut in half.

Heat a little oil in a frying pan/skillet and fry the pancetta until crisp. Drain on paper towels. Layer the fillings in the two sandwiches, starting with the pancetta, then follow with the goat's cheese, peperoncini and rocket/arugula, finishing with the sun-blush tomatoes.

Brush both sides of the panini with oil and toast in the preheated panini press for 3 minutes, or according to the manufacturer's instructions. The bread should be golden brown and the filling warmed through.

Bologna, the gastronomic capital of Italy, is renowned for its mortadella, a silky-textured mammoth salami. Salty Provolone cheese and giardiniera (little pickled vegetables) balance the flavours. You can buy giardiniera in small jars or try making your own.

mortadella, provolone and giardiniera panini

1 ciabatta loaf
4 thin slices of mortadella
4 tablespoons chopped
   Giardiniera (see page 140)
2 small handfuls of rocket/
   arugula
80 g/3 oz. Provolone cheese,
   thinly sliced
vegetable oil, for brushing

MAKES 2 PANINI

Preheat a panini press. Cut the top and bottom off the ciabatta so that it is about 3 cm/1 inch high. Save the crusts for another use. Slice open lengthways and then cut in half.

Layer the fillings in the two sandwiches, starting with the mortadella, and then adding the giardiniera and rocket/arugula, finishing with the cheese. Brush both sides of the panini with oil and toast in the preheated panini press for 3 minutes, or according to the manufacturer's instructions. The bread should be golden brown and the filling warmed through.

Serving suggestion: Try serving this panino with a crisp green salad on the side.

This 'pizzaiola panini' makes the ideal snack for lovers of authentic Italian pizza.

pepperoni, mozzarella, black olive and pesto panini

1 ciabatta loaf

2 tablespoons tomato purée/paste

2 tablespoons Basil Pesto (see page 139)

12 small thin slices of pepperoni sausage

10 black olives, pitted and sliced

8 thinly sliced rings of red onion

130 g/5 oz. (2 large balls) fresh buffalo mozzarella, sliced

vegetable oil, for brushing

MAKES 2 PANINI

Preheat a panini press. Cut the top and bottom off the ciabatta so that it is about 3 cm/1 inch high. Save the crusts for another use. Slice open lengthways and then cut in half.

Spread one half of each sandwich with tomato purée/paste and the other side with pesto. Layer the fillings, starting with the pepperoni, followed by the olives and onion, finishing with the cheese. Brush both sides of the panini with oil and toast in the preheated panini press for 3 minutes, or according to the manufacturer's instructions. The bread should be golden brown and the filling warmed through.

Serving suggestion: Serve this with a radicchio and shaved fennel side salad.

Pancetta is delicious unsmoked Italian bacon. Its subtle taste and wafer-thin crispness ensure that it enhances but doesn't dominate the other ingredients.

pancetta, gorgonzola and apple panini

1 ciabatta loaf
6 slices pancetta
2 teaspoons balsamic
  vinegar
½ tart green apple, thinly
  sliced
a small handful of rocket/
  arugula
80 g/3 oz. Gorgonzola
  cheese, crumbled
80 g/3 oz. Taleggio or
  Fontina cheese, sliced
sea salt and freshly ground
  black pepper
vegetable oil, for frying and
  brushing

MAKES 2 PANINI

Preheat a panini press. Cut the top and bottom off the ciabatta so that it is about 3 cm/1 inch high. Save the crusts for another use. Slice open lengthways and then cut in half.

Add a little oil to a frying pan/skillet and fry the pancetta until crisp. Drain on paper towels. Drizzle both sandwiches with balsamic vinegar and season with salt and pepper. Layer the fillings in the sandwiches, starting with the pancetta, followed by the apple and rocket/arugula and finishing with the cheeses.

Brush both sides of the panini with oil and toast in the preheated panini press for 3 minutes, or according to the manufacturer's instructions. The bread should be golden brown and the filling warmed through.

This unusual panino has the deliciously mustardy addition of creamed horseradish, which is the natural partner to beef.

roast beef, caramelized onion, watercress and horseradish panini

1 ciabatta loaf
2 tablespoons ready-made creamed horseradish
4 slices of roast beef
4 tablespoons Caramelized Onions (see page 140)
2 handfuls of watercress
60 g/2 oz. Gruyère cheese, sliced
vegetable oil, for brushing

MAKES 2 PANINI

Preheat a panini press. Cut the top and bottom off the ciabatta so that it is about 3 cm/1 inch high. Save the crusts for another use. Slice open lengthways and then cut in half.

Spread the creamed horseradish on the inside of both sandwiches. Layer the fillings, starting with the beef, then the onions and watercress and finish with the cheese. Brush both sides of the panini with oil and toast in the preheated panini press for 3 minutes, or according to the manufacturer's instructions. The bread should be golden brown and the filling warmed through.

Serving suggestion: Serve this panino with a little extra creamed horseradish if you like things hot.

Fontina works beautifully with figs and prosciutto but you could also use mozzarella.

prosciutto, balsamic fig and fontina panini

1 ciabatta loaf
4 slices prosciutto
2–3 ripe figs, sliced
2 teaspoons balsamic
   vinegar
2 handfuls of rocket/arugula
70 g/2½ oz. Fontina cheese,
   sliced
sea salt and freshly ground
   black pepper
vegetable oil, for brushing

MAKES 2 PANINI

Preheat a panini press. Cut the top and bottom off the ciabatta so that it is about 3 cm/1 inch high. Save the crusts for another use. Slice open lengthways and then cut in half.

Divide the prosciutto between the two sandwiches. Top with fig slices, sprinkle with vinegar and season to taste with salt and pepper. Add the rocket/arugula and then the cheese.

Brush both sides of the panini with oil and toast in the preheated panini press for 3 minutes, or according to the manufacturer's instructions. The bread should be golden brown and the filling warmed through.

Other pickled condiments (such as peperoncini) would be equally good here in place of the capers.

salami, roasted fennel, fontina and caper panini

1 ciabatta loaf
8 slices Italian salami
4 slices of Roasted Fennel, roughly chopped (see page 138)
8 thinly sliced rings of red onion
2 teaspoons small capers
80 g/3 oz. Fontina cheese, sliced
vegetable oil, for brushing

MAKES 2 PANINI

Preheat a panini press. Cut the top and bottom off the ciabatta so that it is about 3 cm/1 inch high. Save the crusts for another use. Slice open lengthways and then cut in half.

Layer the salami, fennel, onion, capers and then cheese in both sandwiches. Brush both sides of the panini with oil and toast in the preheated panini press for 3 minutes, or according to the manufacturer's instructions. The bread should be golden brown and the filling warmed through.

Serving suggestion: Try this panino with the Lemon and Fennel Seed Mayonnaise on page 141 for dipping.

Put your leftover turkey meat to good use in this deliciously different panino. Jalapeños are an excellent, unexpected partner here, but for a sweet rather than spicy sandwich, replace them with cranberry relish.

turkey, gruyère, jalapeño and mustard panini

1 ciabatta loaf
3 tablespoons grainy
   mustard
100 g/3½ oz. Gruyère or
   Emmental cheese, sliced
2 tablespoons pickled
   jalapeño slices, drained
4 thick slices of turkey
vegetable oil, for brushing

MAKES 2 PANINI

Preheat a panini press. Cut the top and bottom off the ciabatta so that it is about 3 cm/1 inch high. Save the crusts for another use. Slice open lengthways and then cut in half.

Spread the mustard over the inside of each sandwich. Top with the cheese, follow with the jalapeños and finish with the turkey. Brush both sides of the panini with oil and toast in the preheated panini press for 3 minutes, or according to the manufacturer's instructions. The bread should be golden brown and the filling warmed through.

Serving suggestion: Try serving this panino with the Mustard and Shallot Mayonnaise on page 141 for dipping, and with a simple tomato and red onion side salad.

When melted, Dutch Gouda cheese becomes velvety and gooey, making it the ideal cheese for panini.

chicken, gouda and red onion panini with honey-mustard dressing

1 ciabatta loaf
2 tablespoons ready-made honey-mustard dressing
1 cooked chicken breast
8 thinly sliced rings of red onion
2 handfuls of rocket/arugula
80 g/3 oz. Gouda cheese, sliced
vegetable oil, for brushing

MAKES 2 PANINI

Preheat a panini press. Cut the top and bottom off the ciabatta so that it is about 3 cm/1 inch high. Save the crusts for another use. Slice open lengthways and then cut in half.

Spread the honey-mustard dressing on the inside of both sandwiches. Slice the chicken into four pieces lengthways. Layer the fillings in the two sandwiches starting with the chicken, followed by the onion and rocket/arugula, finishing with the cheese. Brush both sides of the panini with oil and toast in the preheated panini press for 3 minutes, or according to the manufacturer's instructions. The bread should be golden brown and the filling warmed through.

Serving suggestion: Serve this panino with extra honey-mustard dressing on the side for dipping.

Scamorza is smoked mozzarella cheese. It has a more pronounced flavour and firmer texture than the fresh variety. Sun-blush tomatoes can be substituted for the roasted tomatoes if you are short of time.

chicken, scamorza, roasted tomato and watercress panini

1 ciabatta loaf
1 cooked chicken breast
4 slices Roasted Tomatoes
   (see page 138)
2 handfuls of watercress
80 g/3 oz. Scamorza cheese,
   sliced
vegetable oil, for brushing

MAKES 2 PANINI

Preheat a panini press. Cut the top and bottom off the ciabatta so that it is about 3 cm/1 inch high. Save the crusts for another use. Slice open lengthways and then cut in half.

Slice the chicken into 4 pieces lengthways. Layer two slices in each sandwich and follow with the tomatoes, watercress and then the cheese. Brush both sides of the panini with oil and toast in the preheated panini press for 3 minutes, or according to the manufacturer's instructions. The bread should be golden brown and the filling warmed through.

Serving suggestion: Try the Fresh Herb Mayonnaise on page 141 for dipping or add a drizzle of balsamic vinegar.

This is the Italian equivalent of Mexican tacos but turned upside down. The crisply fried polenta bases remain soft in the middle and are topped with chunky guacamole and smokey pan-grilled strips of chicken. The contrast of flavours and textures is amazing.

350 g/¾ lb. skinless,
 boneless chicken breasts
2 tablespoons freshly
 squeezed lemon juice
1 garlic clove, crushed
2 tablespoons olive oil
1 quantity Polenta Crostini
 (see page 9)
butter, for frying, or olive oil
 or melted butter, for
 brushing

FOR THE GUACAMOLE:
2 ripe avocados
6 spring onions/scallions,
 chopped
1 medium tomato, skinned,
 seeded and chopped
2 tablespoons chopped
 fresh coriander/cilantro
lemon juice
sea salt and freshly ground
 black pepper

TO SERVE:
3 cherry tomatoes, halved
coriander/cilantro leaves

SERVES 6

pan-grilled chicken and guacamole on crisp polenta crostini

Cut the chicken into finger-thin strips and mix with the lemon juice, garlic and olive oil. Set aside while you make the guacamole.

Halve the avocados, remove the stones/pits and peel off the skin. Place the flesh in a bowl and mash to a rough texture with a fork. Mix in the spring onions/scallions, chopped tomato and coriander/cilantro. Season to taste with lemon juice, salt and pepper. Don't make this too far in advance as it discolours quickly.

To cook the polenta crostini, melt a little butter in a hot, non-stick frying pan/skiller and cook until crisp, turning once. Alternatively, brush both sides with olive oil or melted butter and pan-grill, turning once, for a char-grilled taste.

To cook the chicken, heat a stovetop grill pan until smoking. Add the chicken strips and pan-grill on one side only for 2–3 minutes, without moving, until cooked.

Spread the crostini with some guacamole then top with chicken strips. Top each one with half a cherry tomato and some coriander/cilantro leaves. Serve immediately.

This combination of caramelized figs and crisply barbecued prosciutto is irresistible. The figs are best cooked on a barbecue, but you can use a stovetop grill pan or a grill – just get the right amount of charring on the figs.

grilled fig and prosciutto bruschetta with rocket/arugula

4 thick slices country bread, preferably sourdough
2 garlic cloves, halved
extra virgin olive oil, for drizzling, plus extra for brushing
8 ripe fresh figs
2 tablespoons balsamic vinegar
12 slices prosciutto
100 g/1 cup rocket/arugula
sea salt and freshly ground black pepper
shavings of Parmesan cheese, to serve

SERVES 4

To make the bruschetta, grill, toast or pan-grill the bread on both sides until lightly charred or toasted. Rub the top side of each slice with the cut garlic, then drizzle with olive oil. Keep them warm in a low oven.

Take the figs and stand them upright. Using a small, sharp knife, make two cuts across each fig not quite quartering it, but keeping it intact at the base. Ease the figs open and brush with balsamic vinegar and olive oil. Put the figs cut-side down on a preheated barbecue or stovetop grill pan and cook for 3–4 minutes until hot and slightly charred – don't move them during cooking. Alternatively, place the figs cut-side up under a really hot grill/broiler until browning and heated through.

While the figs are cooking, place half the slices of prosciutto on the barbecue or stove-top grill pan, or under the grill/broiler and cook until frazzled. Remove and keep warm while cooking the remaining slices. Place two figs, three pieces of prosciutto and some rocket/arugula on each slice of bruschetta. Cover with Parmesan shavings and drizzle with olive oil. Serve immediately.

This pretty-coloured substantial snack has its origins in Spain. The secret ingredient is a mild smoked paprika called pimentón, which gives the potatoes an interesting depth of flavour. If you can't get hold of it, use sweet paprika instead.

chorizo with crunchy saffron potatoes on bruschetta

350 g/¾ lb. potatoes

4 thick slices country bread, preferably sourdough

2 garlic cloves, halved

extra virgin olive oil, for drizzling

2–3 tablespoons sunflower oil

a large pinch saffron threads soaked in 3 tablespoons hot water for 15 minutes

½ teaspoon ground cumin

½ teaspoon pimentón (smoked paprika)

175 g/6 oz. chorizo, sliced or cubed

sea salt and freshly ground black pepper

freshly chopped coriander/cilantro, to serve

SERVES 4

Peel the potatoes and cut into 2.5 cm/1 inch cubes. Cook in boiling salted water for 5–7 minutes until they are almost cooked but still slightly firm in the middle.

While the potatoes are cooking, make the bruschetta. Grill, toast or pan-grill the bread on both sides until lightly charred or toasted. Rub the top side of each slice with the cut garlic, then drizzle with olive oil. Keep them warm in a low oven.

Drain the potatoes well. Heat the sunflower oil in a large frying pan/skillet, add the potatoes and fry them over a medium heat for about 5 minutes, turning from time to time, until a light golden brown. Sprinkle over the saffron water and continue to cook for 3–4 minutes. Next, add the ground cumin and pimentón and cook for a further 5 minutes, tossing and turning the potatoes until they build up a nice spicy crust. Add the chorizo and cook for another 5 minutes until it is heated through.

Season well with salt and pepper, then spoon the mixture over the bruschetta. Sprinkle with freshly chopped coriander/cilantro and serve immediately.

These are delicious mouthfuls of melting mozzarella swathed in Parma ham. They taste good served cold with the addition of a thin slice of ripe melon on top, but heating them up transforms them.

prosciutto-wrapped bocconcini crostini

1 Italian sfilatino or thin French baguette, sliced into thin rounds

extra virgin olive oil, for brushing

24 fresh sage leaves, plus extra to serve

24 bocconcini cheeses or 3 regular mozzarella cheeses, cubed

8 slices prosciutto or Parma ham

3 tablespoons grain mustard

1 teaspoon balsamic vinegar

sea salt and freshly ground black pepper

SERVES 6

Preheat the oven to 190°C (375°F) Gas 5. To make the crostini, brush both sides of each slice of bread with olive oil and spread out on a baking sheet. Bake for about 10 minutes until crisp and golden. Let cool, then keep in an airtight container until ready to use. It is best to reheat them in the oven before adding the topping.

Put a sage leaf on top of each bocconcini or mozzarella cube and season with salt and pepper. Cut each slice of ham into three equal pieces and wrap up a piece of cheese in each one.

Mix the mustard and balsamic vinegar together and spread on the crostini. Pop two mozzarella parcels on top of each crostini and put on a baking sheet. Bake in the oven for 3–5 minutes or until the cheese just melts. Serve the crostini immediately, topped with more sage leaves.

4 thick slices of country
  bread, preferably
  sourdough
2 garlic cloves, halved
extra virgin olive oil, for
  drizzling
225 g/½ lb. best fillet/
  tenderloin of beef,
  perfectly trimmed
100 g/1 cup rocket/arugula
sea salt and freshly ground
  black pepper
shavings of Parmesan
  cheese, to serve

FOR THE SALSA VERDE:
1 teaspoon sea salt
2 garlic cloves, finely
  chopped
4 anchovy fillets in oil,
  rinsed
3 tablespoons freshly
  chopped parsley
3 tablespoons freshly
  chopped mint
3 tablespoons freshly
  chopped basil
2 tablespoons salted capers,
  rinsed and chopped
150 ml/⅔ cup cold-pressed
  extra virgin olive oil, plus
  extra for sealing
2 tablespoons lemon juice
freshly ground black pepper

SERVES 4

This colourful dish relies on using the best beef fillet you can buy, thinly sliced and served with the classic Italian caper and herb sauce.

carpaccio of beef with salsa verde on bruschetta

To make the salsa verde, pound the salt and garlic with a mortar and pestle until creamy. Stir in the anchovies, parsley, mint, basil, capers, olive oil, lemon juice and pepper. Transfer to a jar and pour a layer of olive oil on top to exclude the air. This will keep for up to a week in the refrigerator.

To make the bruschetta, grill, toast or pan-grill the bread on both sides until lightly charred or toasted. Rub the top side of each slice with the cut garlic, then drizzle with olive oil. Keep them warm in a low oven.

Wrap the beef tightly in clingfilm/plastic wrap and put into the freezer for 20 minutes or until just beginning to freeze. Using a very sharp, thin-bladed knife, slice the beef into paper-thin slices (the part-freezing will make this easier). If you find this difficult, cut it as thinly as you can, then bat it out between two sheets of clingfilm/plastic wrap, without breaking through the flesh. This should be done at the last minute, or the meat will discolour.

Brush the bruschetta with a little salsa verde, then drape the sliced beef over the top. Spoon on some more salsa verde and top with a mound of rocket/arugula and a few Parmesan shavings. Season with salt and pepper and serve immediately.

There is nothing more delicious on a cool autumnal evening than a golden polenta crostoni fried or grilled until crisp, topped with succulent Italian pork sausage, covered with melting Taleggio cheese and sweetly soft radicchio. You could be in front of a roaring fire in the Tuscan hills.

italian sausage with radicchio and taleggio on crisp polenta crostoni

1 quantity Polenta Crostini
  (see page 9)
butter, for frying, or olive oil
  or melted butter, for
  brushing
1 small radicchio
2 tablespoons olive oil, for
  brushing
4 fat Italian pork sausages
  (or any other high-meat
  content butcher's
  sausage)
100–150 g/4–5 oz. Taleggio
  or Fontina cheese (or
  other nutty quick-melting
  cheese)
8 fresh sage leaves
sea salt and freshly ground
  black pepper

SERVES 4

Preheat a frying pan/skillet, grill or stove-top grill pan. Cut the polenta into four thick slices, slightly smaller than the size of your hand (these are now crostoni). To cook the polenta crostoni, melt a little butter in a hot, non-stick frying pan/skillet and cook until crisp, turning once. Alternatively, brush both sides of the crostoni with olive oil or melted butter and grill or pan-grill on both sides.

Quarter the radicchio and remove the bitter white core. Put the leaves cut side up on a preheated stovetop grill pan. Brush with olive oil and season with salt and pepper. Add the sausages to the pan and pan-grill for about 10 minutes until the sausages are cooked and the radicchio has softened and is a little charred.

Meanwhile, remove the rind from the cheese and slice thickly. Slice the cooked sausages thickly, too. Put the cooked polenta slices on a lined grill/broiler pan and cover with the sausage slices. Top each crostoni with a couple of sage leaves then a piece of radicchio, then cover each one with a layer of sliced cheese. Place under a hot grill/broiler and grill/broil until the cheese is melted and bubbling. Serve immediately.

A classic Italian restaurant favourite, but this more rustic version is so easy to make at home. The mozzarella melts inside the crisp bread coat, revealing a surprise of sun-dried tomatoes and ham inside.

mozzarella and ham in carozza

2 mozzarella cheeses, thickly sliced

8 thin oval slices country bread

8 sun-dried tomatoes, soaked until soft and cut into strips

4 slices Prosiutto Cotto or other mild ham

2 teaspoons dried oregano

3 eggs, beaten

vegetable oil, for shallow frying

sea salt and freshly ground black pepper

SERVES 4

Arrange the mozzarella slices over 4 of the slices of bread. Arrange the sun-dried tomatoes, ham slices and oregano over the mozzarella. Season well with salt and pepper, then put the remaining bread slices on top. Press down well.

Pour the beaten eggs into a large dish and dip the sandwiches in the egg, turning once to coat both sides. Leave them to soak up the egg for 30 minutes.

Heat the oil in a deep frying pan/skillet until a crumb dropped in sizzles instantly. Fry each sandwich for 1–2 minutes on each side until crisp and golden brown. Drain on paper towels and serve piping hot.

Melting cheese oozes around spheres of seasoned beef to perfection.

1 large ciabatta, cut into
   3 thick slices then cut
   widthways
4–6 slices or about 250 g/
   3 cups grated Fontina

meatball panini with tomato sauce & fontina

FOR THE MEATBALLS:
225 g/8 oz. minced/ground
   meat, half beef and half
   Italian sausage
30 g/½ cup fresh
   breadcrumbs
1 teaspoon dried oregano
1 teaspoon dried rosemary
a pinch of dried chilli
   flakes/hot pepper flakes
1 egg, beaten
2 tablespoons milk, or more
   if necessary
1 teaspoon salt
freshly ground black pepper

Preheat the oven to 190°C (375°F) Gas 5. Line a baking sheet with parchment paper. In a mixing bowl, combine all the meatball ingredients and form into 8–10 golf ball-sized balls. Arrange on the baking sheet and bake until browned and cooked though, 20–30 minutes. Let cool slightly. Slice in half and set aside until needed.

Meanwhile, prepare the sauce. Coat the garlic cloves lightly with oil, place in a small ovenproof dish and roast, at the same time as the meatballs, for 10–15 minutes, until golden and tender. Do not let the garlic burn. Remove the garlic from the oven, slip the cloves from their skins and chop finely. In a small saucepan, melt the butter. Add the passata/strained tomatoes, garlic, sugar and salt and pepper. Simmer for 15 minutes. Taste and adjust seasoning. Keep warm until needed.

FOR THE SAUCE:
3 garlic cloves, crushed but
   not peeled
extra virgin olive oil
200 g/7 oz. passata/strained
   tomatoes
1 tablespoon unsalted butter
a pinch of sugar
sea salt and ground black
   pepper

SERVES 2

Coat the outsides of the bread slices with oil. If space allows, put the three slices of bread, oil-side down, in a large frying pan/skillet. Arrange half the cheese slices on top of each slice, then top with the meatball halves, dividing the pieces evenly between the two sandwiches. Coat the inside of the remaining bread pieces generously with the tomato sauce and place on top. Turn the heat to medium and cook the first side for 3–4 minutes, pressing gently with a spatula. Carefully turn with a large spatula and cook on the other side for 2–3 minutes or until deep golden brown all over.

Let cool for a few minutes before serving with a small wooden skewer through the middle to hold the sandwich together.

The authentic version of this sandwich calls for melted cheese to top the meat and onions, so grilling it is a departure from tradition. This recipes uses both Swiss cheese or processed cheese.

philly cheese steak panini

2 large onions, thinly sliced
15 g/1 tablespoon unsalted
  butter
3 tablespoons vegetable oil
350 g/¾ lb. minute/cube
  steak, thinly sliced
1 ciabatta
3 tablespoons spreadable
  processed cheese, such as
  Dairylea or Kraft
6–8 slices Emmental or
  other Swiss cheese
2 large gherkins/pickles,
  thinly sliced lengthways,
  plus extra to serve
sea salt and freshly ground
  black pepper

SERVES 2

In a frying pan/skillet, combine the onions with the butter and 2 tablespoons of the vegetable oil. Cook over a medium heat, stirring occasionally, until deep golden brown, about 10 minutes. Season lightly and transfer to a small bowl.

In the same pan/skillet, add another 1 tablespoon oil and heat. When hot but not smoking, add the beef and cook for 2–3 minutes, stirring often until cooked through. Season lightly and set aside.

To assemble, cut the ciabatta in half at the middle to obtain two even pieces, and slice these in half widthways. Spread the inside of the bottom slice of each half with a portion of the processed cheese. With a small brush, coat the outsides of the bread lightly, on both sides, with oil.

If space allows, put the plain slices of bread, oil-side down, in a large frying pan/skillet. Arrange half the Emmental slices on top, then top with half the beef and half the onions. Cover with the processed cheese-coated bread slice and place on top of the sandwich to enclose, oil-side up. Turn the heat to medium and cook the first side for 3–5 minutes, pressing gently with a large spatula. Carefully turn with the spatula and cook on the other side, for 2–3 minutes or until deep golden brown all over.

Cut in half and leave to cool for a few minutes before serving. Repeat for the remaining sandwich if necessary.

4
Dolci Sweet Treats

kirsch-soaked cherry and nectarine panini with cream cheese and almonds

·

raspberry and mascarpone brioche panini

·

nutella and banana brioche panini

Cherries are delicious here but you can try any other fruit that's in season at the same time, such as strawberries.

kirsch-soaked cherry and nectarine panini with cream cheese and almonds

4 thick slices brioche bread
12 fresh cherries, stoned/ pitted
1 nectarine, stoned/pitted and thinly sliced
1 tablespoon kirsch
4 tablespoons cream cheese
2 tablespoons flaked/ slivered almonds, lightly toasted
1 tablespoon Demerara sugar
vegetable oil, for brushing

MAKES 2 PANINI

Preheat a panini press. Put the cherries and nectarine slices in a large bowl, add the kirsch and toss gently. Spread the cream cheese on two of the slices of brioche. Press the cherries and nectarines on top and then sprinkle with the almonds and sugar. Top with the other two pieces of bread and press them together.

Brush both sides of the panini with a little oil and toast in the preheated panini press for 2 minutes, or according to the manufacturer's instructions. The bread should be golden brown and the filling warmed through.

Rethink dessert with this simple but stellar panini. Use white bread with the crusts removed if you can't find brioche.

raspberry and mascarpone brioche panini

4 thick slices brioche bread
4 tablespoons mascarpone
2 handfuls of raspberries
2 teaspoons Demerara sugar
vegetable oil, for brushing

SERVES 2

Spread two slices of the bread with the mascarpone cheese. Place the raspberries on top and sprinkle with the sugar. Top both sandwiches with the second slice. Brush both sides of the panini with a little oil and toast in the preheated panini press for 2 minutes, or according to the manufacturer's instructions. The bread should be golden brown and the filling warmed through.

Serving suggestion: Alternatively, try this panini with thin slices of fresh strawberries instead of the raspberries.

Children (and adults) around the world are grateful for one of Italy's biggest exports – Nutella. This luxurious chocolate spread made with hazelnuts and chocolate is marvellous just scooped up and devoured by the spoonful. But when warmed up between two pieces of brioche with some banana it becomes something sublime!

nutella and banana brioche panini

4 thick slices brioche bread
4 tablespoons Nutella or other chocolate-hazelnut spread
1 small banana, thinly sliced
vegetable oil, for brushing

SERVES ?

Preheat a panini press. Spread 2 slices of the brioche with the Nutella. Place the banana slices on top. Close the sandwiches with the second slice of brioche. Brush both sides of the panini with a little oil and toast in the preheated panini press for 2 minutes, or according to the manufacturer's instructions. The bread should be golden brown and the filling warmed through.

Serving suggestion: As an alternative, try replacing the Nutella with a good-quality wholenut peanut butter.

5
Condimenti
Relishes & Mayos

roasted tomatoes

•

roasted fennel

•

basil pesto

•

sun-blush tomato pesto

•

caramelized onions

•

giardiniera

•

homemade mayonnaise

roasted tomatoes

6 large Italian plum
  tomatoes
2 garlic cloves, thickly sliced
1 teaspoon sea salt
½ teaspoon cracked black
  pepper
2 tablespoons olive oil
1 tablespoon balsamic
  vinegar

MAKES 12 HALVES

These are wonderful in just about any recipe, from pasta to pizza.

Preheat the oven to 170°C (325°F) Gas 3. Slice the tomatoes in half lengthways. Place in a large roasting pan lined with foil. Sprinkle the garlic, salt and pepper over and drizzle with olive oil. Bake in the preheated oven for 45 minutes. Remove, drizzle with vinegar and let sit for 10 minutes. When cool, pack into an airtight container. Once sealed, the tomatoes will keep in the fridge for up to 1 week.

roasted fennel

Liquorice-flavoured fennel becomes very sweet when roasted. A little boiling water in the pan keeps the flesh soft while the edges crisp up and caramelize.

4 large fennel bulbs
2 garlic cloves, thickly sliced
1 teaspoon sea salt
½ teaspoon cracked black
  pepper
2 tablespoons olive oil
1 tablespoon balsamic
  vinegar

MAKES 8–10 SLICES

Preheat the oven to 170°C (325°F) Gas 3. Cut the fennel in half lengthways and cut the core out. Slice the pieces about 1.5 cm/1/2 inch thick and place in a large roasting pan lined with foil. Sprinkle the garlic, salt and pepper over and drizzle with olive oil. Put the fennel in the preheated oven to roast for 1 hour. About 15 minutes into the cooking time pour 125 ml/1/2 cup boiling water into the pan. When cooked, drizzle with the vinegar. Once cool, pack in an airtight container. Once sealed the fennel will keep in the fridge for up to 1 week.

basil pesto

Jarred pesto just doesn't have the same heady aroma as homemade. If you buy it then look for brands that are made with 100 per cent olive oil.

1 large garlic clove, crushed
100 g/3½ oz. pine nuts, toasted
2 bunches basil, leaves only
200 ml/⅔ cup extra virgin olive oil
100 g/3½ oz. Parmesan cheese, grated
sea salt

MAKES 400 ML/1⅔ CUPS

Place the garlic, pine nuts and basil in a food processor. Keep the motor running and slowly pour in the olive oil. Scrape the mixture into a bowl and stir in the Parmesan and a small pinch of salt.

Pour the pesto into an airtight container. Once sealed the pesto will keep in the fridge for up to 10 days.

sun-blush tomato pesto

Sun-blush tomatoes are a hybrid between sun-dried and oven-roasted.

150 g/5 oz. sun-blush tomatoes, drained
100 g/3½ oz. pine nuts, toasted
1 garlic clove
60 g/2 oz. Parmesan cheese, grated
1 teaspoon dried chilli flakes/hot pepper flakes
125 ml/½ cup extra virgin olive oil
sea salt and freshly ground black pepper

MAKES 500 ML/2 CUPS

In a food processor combine the tomatoes, pine nuts, garlic, Parmesan and chilli flakes/hot pepper flakes. Keep the motor running and slowly pour in the olive oil. Add salt and pepper to taste. Spoon the pesto into an airtight container. Once sealed the pesto will keep in the fridge for up to 1 week.

caramelized onions

You can buy jars of caramelized onion jam but homemade are much tastier.

3 tablespoons olive oil
2 large onions, cut into thin
   slices
1 tablespoon red wine
   vinegar
1 teaspoon sugar
1 teaspoon sea salt
½ teaspoon cracked black
   pepper

MAKES 350 G/³/₄ LB.

Heat the oil in a large frying pan/skillet. Add the onions, salt and pepper and fry for 3 minutes over high heat. Turn the heat down to medium/low and fry for 20 minutes more. Add the vinegar and sugar and cook for 5 more minutes. Remove from the heat.

When cool, spoon into an airtight container. Refrigerate for up to 1 week.

½ a small head cauliflower
1 red pepper, deseeded
2 medium carrots
2 celery sticks/ribs, sliced
40 g/1½ oz. Sicilian green
   olives, stoned/pitted
30 g/1 oz. peperoncini

PICKLING LIQUID:
300 ml/1¼ cups white wine
   vinegar
350 ml/1½ cups water
75 g/⅓ cup sugar
2½ tablespoons sea salt
a pinch of dried chilli/hot
   red pepper flakes
½ teaspoon yellow mustard
   seeds

MAKES 350 G/³/₄ LB.

giardiniera

Do try these delicious little pickles.

Heat the oil in a large frying pan/skillet. Add the onions, salt and pepper and fry for 3 minutes over high heat. Turn the heat down to medium/low and fry for 20 minutes more. Add the vinegar and sugar and cook for 5 more minutes. Remove from the heat.

When cool, spoon into an airtight container. Refrigerate for up to 1 week.

homemade mayonnaise

Serve your panini with this delicious homemade mayonnaise on the side.

1 tablespoon Dijon mustard
½ teaspoon sea salt
½ teaspoon white pepper
2 egg yolks, at room
    temperature
200 ml/¾ cup grapeseed or
    sunflower oil
3 tablespoons extra virgin
    olive oil
1 tablespoon freshly
    squeezed lemon juice
1 teaspoon sugar

MAKES 300 ML/1¼ CUPS

VARIATIONS

Simply stir these extra ingredients into the freshly prepared mayonnaise:

Saffron garlic Add 1 teaspoon crushed saffron threads (soaked in 1 tablespoon hot water) and 1 crushed garlic clove.

Caper, chive and onion Add 1 tablespoon each of chopped capers, chives and caramelized onion.

Fresh herb Add 3 tablespoons mixed fresh chopped herbs such as tarragon, parsley, basil, coriander/cilantro, chives or dill.

Orange, olive and parsley Add 1 tablespoon finely grated orange zest, 1 tablespoon chopped black olives and 2 tablespoons chopped parsley.

Smoky paprika Add 1 tablespoon sweet Spanish paprika (pimentón dulce), 1 crushed garlic clove and 1 teaspoon finely grated lemon zest.

Lemon and fennel seed Add the finely grated zest of 1 lemon, 1 tablespoon freshly squeezed lemon juice, 1 teaspoon ground fennel seeds and 1 tablespoon chopped parsley.

Mustard and shallot Add 2 tablespoons grainy mustard, 1 tablespoon Dijon mustard and 1 tablespoon very finely chopped shallot.

index

picture credits

Photography by the following:

Martin Brigdale
Page 136 below

Peter Cassidy
Front cover right, pages 54, 136
above right

Gus Filgate
Front cover below, spine, pages
1, 2 above left & below, 4–9

background, 10 above right &
below, 32–52, 56 above left &
below, 64–72, 74 above left &
below, 98, 110–122

Richard Jung
Page 136 above left

Steve Painter
Front cover left, pages 31, 125, 126

William Reavell
Pages 2 above right, 3, 5 insert, 10
above left, 13–29, 56 above right,
59–63, 74 above right, 77–97,
101–109, 128–135